WHO PUT YOU IN CHARGE?

by

Lesley Hunter

authorHOUSE®

AuthorHouse™ UK Ltd.
500 Avebury Boulevard
Central Milton Keynes, MK9 2BE
www.authorhouse.co.uk
Phone: 08001974150

First published by AuthorHouse 1/18/2010

ISBN: 978-1-4490-3453-5 (sc)

This book is printed on acid-free paper.

FOR

Allan Ramsay Hunter

(1932 – 2005)

CONTENTS

FOREWORD

I am sure that I'm not alone in wondering just what a skilled cat herder might teach business managers. "Bring plenty of fish and catnip" might feature in there somewhere, as well as, "expect much sleeping." Good advice for cats maybe, but not likely to prove to be particularly beneficial in the workplace. And whilst it is probably not the easiest task to master, herding cats is undoubtedly much easier than *leading* cats. After all, cats don't tend to demand leadership; they are far too important and far too independent for that.

In this wonderful little book Lesley shows us what we can learn about leadership. Not from cats, but rather from their domesticated and, as some might say, more intelligent counterparts, dogs.

As an expert in the field of leadership development, Lesley outlines her experiences with a powerful personality in the form of Keno, her boisterous Alsation. As a new addition into her family unit, Keno rapidly demanded training, leadership, respect, and reward. But most importantly, he needed a *pack* with whom he knew that he belonged.

Told with authority, wit and a passion for the subject, Lesley clearly demonstrates parallels between workplace leadership skills and being the head of Keno's pack, whilst guiding us through the key principles that anyone involved in leadership today would do well to study.

Lesley's creed as trainer, leader and dog owner is summarised nicely by her own words, *"Bringing together and leading a group of dogs was therefore no different to leading a group of people – by recognising the strengths and characteristics of each individual, and by consciously choosing to adapt my own behaviour and response, I became an effective leader and got the best out of each of them."*

Andrew T. Austin

ACKNOWLEDGEMENTS

Ken and Keno are my inspiration. Without them, this book would simply not have been possible.

Special thanks to Carol Black, for her continuous encouragement to get what was in my head finally onto paper, and to Craig Bloxham for the cover photography.

Thanks to Michelle Ridley, Andy Shipp and Andrew Binns for their invaluable help and suggestions. Finally, thanks to you for choosing to read this book and I hope you enjoy it.

1

SETTING THE SCENE

At some time in your life you will be in charge. Accept it, and get used to it, because it will happen. It might be planned and expected or it might sneak up on you unannounced and you suddenly find yourself in a situation where you are expected to provide leadership to others. Either way, the key question is how well you will rise to the challenge and demonstrate firm and effective leadership.

I had always thought of myself as a strong person and a natural leader. After all, in my early thirties I had taken the brave decision to leave a comfortable well paid full-time job to set up my own business. It never occurred to me that I could fail – and I didn't – because I had a firm resolve from the outset and was clear about what I was doing and why I was doing it. Within twelve months I had a strong and vibrant company that exceeded my original expectations and put me in the position of leading and managing complex projects with over one hundred and twenty staff. Although this was daunting at first, I naturally evolved into the situation and embraced each new challenge as it came along.

Twelve years later, I had sold the company and branched out on my own providing leadership training and development programmes to other businesses. I was confident in my own abilities as a leader. After all, I had taken control of my own life, both personally and professionally, and knew precisely what I wanted and how to get it. I had lived on my own, as an independent individual, for over ten years before marrying Ken and wasn't afraid of taking responsibility for myself, my own decisions and my actions. That was, until Keno (Kee'no) entered my life ...

Keno was born on New Years Eve 2005. He was one of a large litter of German Shepherd puppies but quickly made himself stand out from the crowd. At three weeks old, we visited the breeder to make our choice, which was something I expected to be the hardest decision I would make since I would probably want to take them all home. Oh no ... Keno had other ideas. As we watched his brothers and sisters playing happily with each other, he promptly chewed the laces on my training shoes then climbed into my handbag and went to sleep. I should have seen the warning signs at this first meeting but I simply ignored them because we all fell in love with him in the instant he started snoring cuddled up against my mobile phone.

That's me in the middle...

My Dad was a vet so I had been around dogs all my life. I knew what it meant to be a dog owner and the responsibilities it would bring. However, my husband Ken wasn't quite so well prepared and has had to be a very quick learner!

It was a cold, wet and dark February evening when I drove back to the breeder's house and gently lifted our little bundle of fur into the car. The journey home should have been uneventful. After all, I had an eight week old puppy safely wrapped in a blanket lying in a strong plastic washing basket and I only had to drive six and a half miles. Obviously he had never been in a car before and was a little apprehensive at the start, but within two miles he was feeling a little braver. He was soon up, out of the basket and investigating the gear stick. This was clearly a great game, as I tried to steer with one hand and pick up a wriggling ball of fur and razor sharp teeth with the other. His determination was amazing – every time I put him back in the basket he found another route out – never the same twice. Finally, having wriggled out of my grasp and having wedged himself firmly under the front passenger seat he got bored and started crying pathetically. This was my cue to pull over in the pouring rain, get out of the car, run round to the passenger side and struggle to pull him out – he was quite firmly wedged! I spent the rest of the journey driving home with a wriggling puppy on my knee who seemed fascinated by the windscreen wipers and kept trying to catch them each time they swept in his direction. I thought I had cracked it ... until I clicked on the indicator and gave him such a fright that he promptly emptied his bladder all over my jeans.

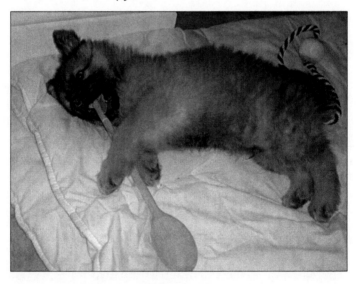

Keno's first night in his new home was relatively uneventful. He settled in quickly and was very affectionate to everyone and everything he encountered. By the end of the evening, his new best friend was a wooden spoon that he was clearly not going to relinquish at bedtime.

I thought I understood what leadership was all about. After all, I trained people in leadership skills and regularly worked with teams that lacked direction and consequently under-performed. So how hard could it be for me to become 'pack leader' to the little ball of fur sitting on my kitchen floor enchanting everyone with his cuteness? Well, I was just about to find out …

Four years on, and I have learned more about leadership and the practical application of leadership skills than I ever thought possible. In fact, when I look back over this time, I wonder how I ever had the audacity to consider myself a successful leader in the first place. Understanding my dog's mind, what makes him tick, and how to develop our working relationship has taken over my life. All the dog training books suggest that an intelligent and strong-willed dog is easy to train – all I can say is they haven't met Keno! At times, it has been a sheer battle of wills. On these occasions, I have devoured every source of help and support available. I have watched every episode of *The Dog Whisperer* (repeatedly) and read every book I can get my hands on. I have frequented canine chat rooms and blogs, and finally undertook the ultimate challenge by enrolling and completing a course in dog training and behavioural practice. Now, I can honestly say that I understand the concepts of leadership more acutely than at any time in my career.

Then something amazing happened. I suddenly realised that dealing with dogs and dealing with people wasn't so different after all and that there was an obvious link between how dogs respond to certain situations and how humans behave. Put simply, I realised that *behaviour is behaviour is behaviour* regardless of where it was being shown. I then spent some time listing the key behaviours I needed to be able to lead Keno effectively and started integrating some of this theory into my leadership development programmes with clients. The response was remarkable. I discovered that people could recognise the patterns of behaviour when they were illustrated using Keno as an example, and could relate to how they would lead and manage the dog. In other words, they already had the leadership strategies they needed, and could articulate them in a different context, but had rarely considered transferring these skills into their work behaviours. My clients were suddenly having 'light bulb' moments where they could clearly see and understand the pattern of why certain things kept happening in their work, and how they could change them. The following chapters illustrate some of these ideas. This is by no means an exhaustive list of skills but then Keno is only four years old and I'm sure I've still got a lot more learning to do!

2

POSITION – POWER PERSUASION

POSITION

The first time I put Keno on a lead was an interesting experience for everyone concerned. He squealed and writhed around as if I was trying to poke him with a hot stick. He made the most horrendous noise that suggested he was being mistreated beyond belief to the point that, after two minutes of ear-splitting screeches and howls, Ken was begging me to stop and remove the collar. "Why can't we do this later when he's a bit older?" he kept asking.

Five minutes later, Keno was happily trotting along the pavement proudly showing off his shiny new collar and lead – walking perfectly and positively bouncing now that he knew what I expected him to do. So what had I actually done?

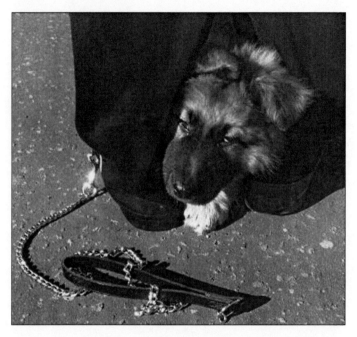

I had asserted my position and made it clear that I was not going to back down until I had achieved my outcome. I had all the power in this relationship because I knew what I was trying to achieve, whereas Keno had no idea what was expected of him. This obviously put him at a disadvantage and I therefore remained calm – despite his gnashing and wailing – and asserted my expectations until he followed my lead (excuse the pun). Quite simply, I had assumed the primary position and made it clear that I was the 'pack leader', thereby providing the direction that Keno needed until he understood what we were trying to achieve. It was important to establish this at the very start and not 'later' as Ken had suggested in order to make sure that Keno began to appreciate the dynamics and relative positions in our relationship.

POWER

Maybe it was the smell of brand new leather or maybe it was the plumpness of the shiny new cushions. From the day it was delivered, Keno obviously assumed the new furniture was intended for him. He had never paid any attention to our old furniture so it didn't occur to me that he would decide the new sofas were being provided specifically for him.

The first time I found him on the sofa he was curled in a tight little ball, snoring gently. He was quickly displaced and told to go to 'bed' while I pointed to the fleece-covered duvet that he had slept on for the last two years. The second time I found him on the sofa he was lying on his back with his right front leg extended either doing an impersonation of Superman or practising Pilates, a position he assumes regularly and which he obviously finds very comfortable.

Although his position was initially funny and caused a few chuckles, I wasn't so gentle this time – he was promptly dumped onto the floor and told to go to 'bed'. At this point he looked at me quizzically and simply climbed back on to the sofa!

There was no doubt that Keno's action was a direct challenge to my authority. I therefore had two options – give in and accept claw scratches on the leather and dog hairs all over my new furniture or make my position absolutely clear and use all my powers of persuasion to set the boundaries. I'm not going to suggest that it was easy … it took several weeks before he finally realised that every time I caught him on the sofa he would be forcefully ejected and sent to bed. The consistency of my approach was crucial to its success by continuing to make my expectations clear. We have obviously reached an understanding because he now only sleeps on the sofa when I am out at work! He thinks I don't know because when I come home, by the time I have opened the front door, he is sitting beautifully on his bed at the foot of the stairs, but the warm dog-shaped dent in the leather is a bit of a giveaway!

Keno doesn't know it yet but he's in for an even bigger surprise … I've just bought a new doorknob for the living room door and am about to exert my power to control the situation and change his behaviour once and for all. I know he'll look for an alternative option but I am confident that he won't go on the beds because he's not allowed upstairs – this has been a rigid rule since he was a tiny puppy. So now all I have to do is stop him climbing onto the hammock every time he goes into the garden!

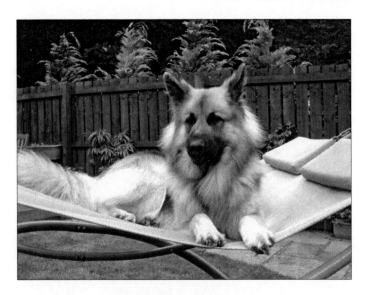

PERSUASION

Having a bath wasn't a problem when Keno was tiny. I simply picked him up, put him into the bath and turned on the taps, which he obviously quite enjoyed as he kept trying to drink the water as it came out. The problem was he soon got too big and too heavy for me to physically lift in to the bath and he made it blatantly clear (by sitting down and refusing to move) that he wasn't going to climb in by himself. So there had to be another way – how was I going to persuade this dog to have a bath?

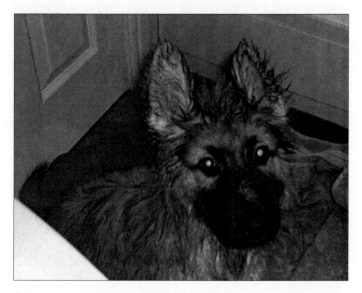

A friend soon came to my aid with an innovative suggestion. Her husband had an old plastic plasterer's trough at the back of his garage that he knew would come in handy one day. Add a beautiful sunny afternoon and a hosepipe and I had my solution. Keno took to it immediately – I think he thought it was a paddling pool. Without realising it at the time, by making the activity fun and enjoyable, I had motivated and encouraged Keno to have a bath. I now consciously persuade him to bathe regularly by simply picking up the hosepipe and filling his trough, which comes in very handy as he has developed a liking for surfing in muddy puddles.

LEADERSHIP LESSONS

In the dog's world, the 'pack leader' is dominant. They earn their position in the pack then accept the responsibilities of the role, while others respect and follow their lead. In the human world, many people find themselves in leadership positions through promotion, reorganisation and restructuring, or succession planning, without actually aspiring to their position. This is when they often find that being 'in charge' is not what they thought it would be – it is sometimes a thankless task and can often leave the person feeling isolated and insecure in themselves. This in turn, does little to promote positive balanced energy so we start a cycle of question and challenge that leads to instability and shifts the balance of power in the 'pack'.

People who trail around after their dogs or, even worse, allow them to pull from the front and weave from left to right as they choose, have inadvertently allowed the dog to assume 'pack leader' position and have put themselves in the secondary position. This is simply setting up opportunities for problems to happen. How can you control a dog when he is in front of you and decides to attack or go off in a different direction? He will have the momentum while you are already on the back foot and have ground to make up before you start.

Dogs follow strong and decisive 'pack leaders'. They will not tolerate unsteadiness or imbalance, yet humans do this all the time. How many people do you know who complain about their 'boss' or colleagues and lack respect for their decisions and actions? This mismatch generates negative energy that does nothing to establish stable and effective working relationships. Leaders do not need to be out there in front charging around on their white horse leading the troops,

> *Effective leaders are consistent and make their expectations clear.*

but if the leader does not hold the prime position in the eyes of their staff then how can they possibly set the direction for staff to follow? The key is therefore to hold the 'pack leader' position at all times. Adopting this approach – and making your expectations clear – means staff will have trust and respect in your direction and will therefore be more inclined to follow you.

Some people hold the view that there are natural born leaders. This doesn't mean that these people have different genes to the rest of us – it simply means they understand and listen to their natural instincts more

> *Effective leaders motivate and encourage others to achieve the outcomes they want.*

readily than the majority of humans do, and use persuasion rather than dominance and authority to achieve their outcomes. Leaders, who follow their instincts and improvise, when necessary, are more likely to inspire and motivate their staff than those who try to bully, coerce or force others to follow them. The most effective leaders are those who know themselves well enough and are therefore able to adapt and modify their learned habits, behaviours and responses to get the best out of each person and situation.

Position   Always be the 'pack leader'.

Power   Know what you are trying to achieve and believe in it and yourself.

Persuasion   Be flexible and adaptable in your own behaviour.

3

Roles – Responsibilities Relationships

Roles

It soon became clear that Keno understood his role in the household. Initially, his prime function was to keep the back garden free of blackbirds! I can't remember the first time he actually met our resident blackbird, or quite how their love-hate relationship developed, but it gave us all hours of endless amusement to watch him frantically chasing the bird from one side of the garden to the other. He didn't seem to realise that he couldn't fly and kept launching himself into the air only to bounce unceremoniously off the fence as the bird glided gracefully about half an inch above his head to land in the neighbour's tree. If I hadn't known any better, I'd have thought that the bird was actually playing with him.

To make matters worse, two doves also decided to take up residence in our neighbour's tree and decided to get in on the act. They had obviously conspired with the blackbird and consequently did their utmost to taunt and antagonise Keno at every opportunity.

To this day Keno still chases any unsuspecting birds round the garden and takes his role of 'head of security' very seriously. In fact, he has even taken to lying in wait for any unsuspecting birds or intruders ... pretending to be asleep in his bath!

The first time he saw snow was another instance where Keno clearly thought his garden was being invaded! He literally exhausted himself running round the garden doing a passable impersonation of a fluffy snowplough pouncing on the snowflakes as they fell and chasing the snowballs I simply couldn't resist throwing at him.

RESPONSIBILITIES

Keno certainly understands his responsibilities as security provider for the house. It doesn't matter who walks up the drive – the first slight footstep is enough to set him off. The window cleaner appears to be his favourite and, given half a chance, he is out there at the bottom of the ladder barking furiously. However, the aura of responsibility falls apart slightly when you know that what he is really doing is saying 'playtime' and the minute he gets the chance he will be running round the garden with a soapy sponge in his mouth. Although Keno creates an image of raw power that suggests he will eat them alive, regular visitors know that this is all an act and that he is really a big softie … but he is a German Shepherd after all and therefore has a reputation and image to maintain.

Keno's sense of responsibility got him into real trouble one day. He obviously assumed that everything that came through the letter box was a potential threat and therefore had to be neutralised (i.e. chewed to oblivion). This didn't matter too much when it was leaflets for local takeaway restaurants or landscape gardeners but it became a little more serious when he decided to ingest an entire packet of Viagra that one of Ken's colleagues had sent him as a practical joke! The vet saw the funny side and made a few unprintable comments but this episode showed me that we had to become much more responsible owners. I promptly had a mailbox fitted to the outside wall and now my only problem is that the dog propels himself at the window like a guided missile every time the postman rattles the mailbox. To an unsuspecting postman you would think he was a killer and was going to eat you. Honestly, he wouldn't ... just ask the window cleaner.

RELATIONSHIPS

Keno has interesting relationships with our neighbours' dogs. There are two Labradors – his best friend (Trevor) and his arch enemy (Toby). In addition, there are two Spaniels and five Shitsus in the space of six houses. He tolerates the Spaniels as they yap and bounce around him but the Shitsus are another matter – they snarl and bark at everything that passes and could pick a fight in an empty house!

One of the Shitsus lives next door and has made it her mission in life to goad and torment Keno by spitting at him through the fence. Most of the time, he blatantly ignores her. Occasionally, he sits at the fence and looks down his nose at her. But, when he thinks no-one is looking, he lets the true nature of their relationship show and simply tries to eat her! I once caught him with his front leg through a gap in the fence pinning her down like a startled rabbit under a paw the size of her head. When I called him, he simply sat down and pretended nothing had happened and looked the picture of innocence.

LEADERSHIP LESSONS

In every pack a dog has its role. For instance, the 'pack leader' is there to provide direction and to maintain order. And then there are the followers, whose role it is to follow the lead, abide by the rules and work within the structure and framework that is provided for them. Harmony happens when pack leaders and followers fulfil their respective roles and carry out their responsibilities effectively. Disharmony, confusion, chaos and ultimately conflict can happen when the individuals concerned are unclear about their roles and are therefore potentially given the opportunity to abdicate some of their responsibilities.

> *Effective leaders adapt and modify their own habits and responses to get the best from each situation.*

A dog also needs a clear set of responsibilities. For instance, a family pet, who is used to being part of a household and is there to guard the house and play with the family, is unlikely to understand what is expected of it if it is put into a working situation, such as search and rescue. Similarly, dogs trained for specific functions, such as police dogs or guide dogs for

21

the blind, have specific responsibilities that are embedded into their training so that they become second nature to them.

People, like dogs, need to know and understand their roles and responsibilities. If someone is unclear about where their responsibilities start and end then one of several things will happen. Firstly, they will take responsibility for the things they like or want to do. This may be comfortable and convenient for them but often means other areas that are more difficult (or less interesting) are avoided. In a team situation this is often characterised by someone 'not pulling their weight' and is a trigger for relationships to start to break down. So, a clear interpretation of a person's role and the responsibilities attached to it are critical in ensuring that positive and beneficial relationships are maintained.

If people are not clear about their roles or responsibilities then confusion is inevitable. For example, think of a jigsaw puzzle. If each individual is a piece in the puzzle, how do they fit together? What contribution does each individual make to the structure, framework and integrity of the whole puzzle? Without the picture on the front of the box it is much harder to get all the pieces in the right place and working together to create the correct result.

Where roles are unclear and people are unsure of their responsibilities, this is characterised in the second stage (storming phase) of Tuckman's Team Development

Model[1]. It is the classic situation where a group of individuals is brought together but they do not yet have a common shared purpose or understanding of what they are trying to achieve. Consequently, there is a high degree of instability among the team, relationships are often strained and cliques and working alliances begin to form. I am often surprised by the number of experienced leaders who find themselves in a situation where their team is displaying typical characteristics of 'storming' and they don't know why.

The simple fact is that any team, no matter how well led or managed, can flip into the storming phase if certain factors change. Most notably, a significant shift in focus or direction for the team, a new person joining, an established person leaving, or even something as apparently mundane as a change in some of the systems and procedures that underpin the way the team works. An effective leader will demonstrate the capacity to anticipate any changes that are likely to affect their team, and should also have sufficient awareness to appreciate the inevitability of a storming situation, rather than trying to fight against it.

> *Effective leaders have a clear interpretation of each person's role and the responsibilities attached to it.*

A person's role basically defines their function, i.e. what is the purpose of them being there and what contribution do they make to the organisation. However, roles often get confused with an individual's 'identity', particularly in

---

[1] Tuckman, Bruce. "Developmental sequence in small groups". *Psychological Bulletin* **63** (6): 384-99

larger teams or organisations. In other words, people 'take on' the identity of the role they have assumed, such as the boss, the manager, the supervisor, the troublemaker, the quiet one. This attribution of identity to role is not helpful. It increases the chance of misinterpretation and gives greater opportunity for people to bring their own perceptions and prejudices to bear. It also allows people to blur the boundaries between what they are expected to do and what they actually do.

When responsibilities aren't made clear, a typical pattern usually emerges. People instinctively take responsibility for things they like to do and want to do (whether they are within the remit of their role or not) or things they are comfortable doing. They then conveniently avoid the things that they find difficult to do, they don't like doing or they simply don't want to do. This in turn causes several things to happen. Firstly, overlap, where several individuals can appear to be taking responsibility for the same aspect of work. This is inefficient and ineffective, and ultimately leads to confusion. Secondly, gaps occur, where people do not fulfil the responsibilities associated with their role and elements of work are left unattended. How often have you heard someone say, "But that's not part of my job" or "That's not within my remit"? This is how blame cultures arise, where people become suspicious of

> *Effective leaders anticipate where activities will straddle the boundaries of individuals' roles and responsibilities, and will communicate their expectations clearly to ensure no compromise to relationships.*

others and their motives, and there is a consequent negative knock-on effect on relationships. So therefore the roles assigned to individuals and the identified responsibilities that each of those roles carry are inextricably linked with the relationships that will be established and developed in the organisation.

Many of the classic leadership models focus on the balance that a leader places between concern for people (i.e. the relationships within the team) and production (i.e. the outputs from the team's work). In particular, the Blake Mouton Model[2] identifies two extremes and highlights that neither of them has all the elements to produce the desired outcomes. It defines a 'country club' style of

> *Effective leaders anticipate changes that are likely to affect their team and plan with this in mind.*

leadership where the needs and interests of the people are considered more important than the outcomes they are trying to achieve. Although this typically creates a nice working environment, there is often too much emphasis on relationships and too little focus on getting the job done. Conversely, the 'produce or perish' style of leadership has the achievement of outcomes as the paramount factor, often to the detriment of working relationships. Blake and Mouton therefore advocated that effective leaders need to recognise and balance these potentially competing elements, but without simply aiming for a 'middle of the road' compromise.

---

2   Blake, R.; Mouton, J. (1964). *The Managerial Grid: The Key to Leadership Excellence*. Houston: Gulf Publishing Co.

Positive relationships are fundamental to the effective working of a team. Yet surprisingly, few leaders deliberately and specifically take into account the strengths, limitations and characteristics of each individual alongside their roles and responsibilities in order to deliberately foster such relationships. Clearly people should not work in silos and there will be situations where, quite appropriately, individuals' roles and responsibilities will have a degree of overlap. However, the key message is that this has to be made clear from the outset. Clarity will lead to a shared understanding of where the boundaries are and how people are expected to work within and around them, and how this in itself is a positive feature that will benefit ongoing and sustainable working relationships.

An effective leader will make a clear distinction between responsibility and accountability. They will 'anticipate' where any activities or projects are likely to straddle the boundaries of individuals' roles and responsibilities and will plan how this will be communicated and managed with no compromise to relationships.

R oles   Be clear about each individual's purpose, function and contribution to the team.

R esponsibilities Communicate responsibilities (and boundaries) clearly to everyone in the team.

R elationships   Anticipate factors that could affect relationships and clarify your expectations.

4

ATTITUDE – ANTICIPATION ACTION

ATTITUDE

Keno learnt the 'sit' command from an early age. He used it as a party trick to charm relatives and visitors, leaving them all with the impression that he was the best behaved puppy they had ever seen. If only they knew the truth! The minute he didn't have an audience, he reverted to typical behaviour.

Having mastered 'sit' and 'stay', I decided it was now time to learn 'come' and 'heel'. So, armed with my bag of treats (freshly cooked chicken – only the best will do) we ventured out into the garden for a training session. I knew exactly what I wanted to achieve but Keno had other ideas. I told him to 'sit' – he sat. I told him to 'come' – he cocked his head to one side and looked at me as if I was an idiot. I could almost hear him thinking, "Why would I want to do that now that I'm sitting? Make your mind up!" The attitude was dripping out of him like syrup. He then promptly got up, wandered round the garden for a little while then trotted over to me eyeing the bag of chicken hungrily.

In reality, Keno had behaved precisely as I had asked – he just hadn't made the link to combine the two separate commands into one action. Although I had a clear goal that I wanted to achieve, getting there in one step was too much to expect. I had to break it down into smaller steps and tackle each in turn. An hour later and we had both mastered the situation ... I had a dog that would sit and come on command and Keno had a new party trick.

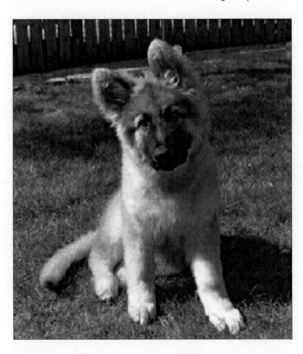

ANTICIPATION

Keno loves going in the car. The simple phrase "in the car" is enough to send him into a frenzy of anticipation. He gets so excited that he bounces around impersonating Tigger and almost turns cartwheels. It doesn't matter what time of day it is; the simple action of suggesting he is going somewhere in the car is enough to trigger mayhem. The embarrassing thing is that he doesn't discriminate between cars – he will simply target the closest vehicle and insert himself through the nearest open door. He has positively bulldozed his way into several of my neighbours' vehicles. They are getting used to it and rapidly close all their doors when they see him bounding across the pavement (another good example of anticipation) but he excelled himself on a recent visit to Ken's work at Police Headquarters!

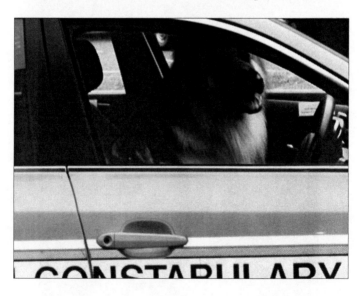

Recently, Keno had to undergo tests for a rare and painful bowel condition and had to make regular visits to the vet. Some of the procedures they carried out were unpleasant and he obviously wasn't particularly happy about being there. On the days of his appointments he would bounce out of the house into the car in his usual enthusiastic way but the minute we turned right at a set of traffic lights in the next village, he instinctively knew where we were going and the pathetic whimpering would start. By the time we reached the surgery, the anticipation of what was likely to happen next had grown to the point where he would be shaking like a jelly. It is so embarrassing to have to drag a dog the size of a small pony into a surgery where other animals are sitting perfectly calm and collected. But this illustrates that anticipation can be both positive and negative, and that the outcomes are often linked to the level of anticipation and the expectation that creates.

Action

By the time he was two years old, Keno had what I considered to be some bad habits and learned behaviours, particularly in relation to other dogs. He had been attacked when he was a puppy (more about this later) and I had assumed that this was the reason he could be unpredictable and occasionally aggressive with other dogs. However, I now know that I was deluding myself and trying to find an excuse, rather than recognising the problem and tackling it with clear and decisive action.

Every time a dog approached Keno and tried to socialise by sniffing his backside (as dogs do) he would become tense and potentially aggressive. Sometimes he reciprocated and they got on fine – other times he would turn and snap sharply at the 'intruder'. I had no way of predicting how he would respond and this in turn made me anxious and often nervous about bringing him into close contact with other dogs – even to the point that I would cross the street rather than take the risk and walk him past another dog on a lead.

When it became apparent that Keno had a hereditary condition that affected his anal glands, I began to realise that there was probably an underlying problem that needed to be resolved. I hadn't made the link between him possibly being in pain around his back end, feeling vulnerable and then simply acting to protect himself from unwanted attention. So, on one of Keno's regular visits to the surgery when the vet explained that, although there was no cure for his condition, castration could make a significant difference and may relieve some pain, I realised I had a decision to make …

Keno was castrated earlier this year. He wasn't particularly happy about it and spent a considerable amount of time seeking sympathy and attention from everyone he met. However, the long-term consequence of my action is that he now has a wonderful time every day running and playing happily with several packs of other dogs. His aggression has all but disappeared and he happily socialises and responds well with other dogs, regardless of whether he knows them or has simply met them for the first time.

Some of my friends and family (particularly my husband and step-son) still think I was cruel to remove Keno's 'equipment' and that I should have bred from him before taking such drastic action. My response is simple. Although my action was unpopular at the time, he is now a much happier and healthier dog, and any hereditary problems have not been passed on to another generation. Sometimes a leader simply has to make decisions that are not particularly comfortable or popular.

LEADERSHIP LESSONS

Dogs live in the moment. They don't fret over their past mistakes or worry about future events – they simply exist and get on with life. Obviously, some behaviour is learned as a response to a stimulus (e.g. Keno's reaction to the postman) but their general behaviour is a direct consequence of their state of mind and is directly linked to their experience of what is happening around them at the time.

Personally I don't believe there is such a thing as 'attitude'. When someone says, "I don't like your attitude" what they are really saying is "I don't like your behaviour" or "I don't like the way you are responding to my behaviour". So, for me, attitude is all about behaviour. It is about perceptions and expectations of other people's behaviours. Put this into the workplace and we are back to the situation where people are 'labelled' with attitude in a similar way to their 'identity' label arising from their perceived role.

Having a 'positive attitude' is often used as a socially acceptable turn of phrase, suggesting that someone has a positive outlook. What is really meant is that the individual concerned is demonstrating a positive resourceful emotional state that is being exhibited through their behaviour. Once you start to look at attitude from the point of behaviour, you will start to recognise patterns in people's behaviour. The patterns that occur most often are the behaviours that have become habitual and these are the ones that people typically don't even know about or recognise in themselves. You will have some; other people will recognise them but you are probably unaware of them unless someone tells you.

> *Effective leaders recognise patterns of behaviour and appreciate that these are often perceived and labelled as 'attitude'.*

As a leader, how do you use an understanding of behavioural patterns to make sure that you develop a positive resourceful 'attitude'? If attitude is a perception and interpretation of behaviour and if behaviour has a neurological and a physiological aspect to it, then having the skill to be able to read an individual's physiology (often referred to as body language or non-verbal cues) is a powerful skill for any leader to master. It is also just as important to understand and recognise how your own emotional states affect your neurology and physiology, and how you exhibit this in your patterns of behaviour.

Feedback is an important mechanism here. When Joseph Luft and Harry Ingham developed their concept of The Johari Window[3] in the 1950s, they basically identified that

> *Effective leaders appreciate the value of feedback.*

people are 'blind' to some of their own behaviours that others recognise in them. Taking this a stage further suggests that unless we actively ask and solicit feedback from others (or they opt to tell us anyway) then we are unlikely to be aware of some of our own behaviours and their impact. When did you last deliberately request some feedback on your behaviour in the workplace and ask how this contributed to your performance and the overall effectiveness of the team or organisation?

Some people call this 'appraisal' or 'performance management' but in too many organisations these processes are either ineffective tick-box exercises or are seen as once-

3   Luft, J.; Ingham, H. (1955). "The Johari window, a graphic model of interpersonal awareness". *Proceedings of the western training laboratory in group development* (Los Angeles: UCLA).

a-year events that have little direct bearing on everyday working practice. The most effective leaders appreciate the value of feedback in terms of understanding the underlying patterns of behaviour and how this links to peoples' perceptions of attitude.

Anticipation! For me, this is the difference that really makes the difference between average and effective leaders. We all have the ability to learn from our mistakes but the most effective leaders not only learn from previous experiences but also use the knowledge and insight they have gained to anticipate potential scenarios and have plans and strategies in place to react accordingly. They have constantly got one eye on the future and are asking themselves, "What if?" Anticipation is therefore the key to effective leadership.

> *Effective leaders recognise the power of anticipation, and that the outcomes are often linked to the level of anticipation and the expectation it creates.*

Anticipation creates a framework for decision making. It provides flexibility, adaptability and the opportunity for choice. This holds true for events, behaviours, changes in circumstances and changes in dynamics, all of which have a subsequent knock-on effect on the work and productivity of individuals, teams and organisations. As an effective leader, you will recognise the signs and symptoms, have contingency plans in place and therefore be able to react faster, respond more flexibly and intervene more quickly to capitalise on opportunities and minimise any potential implications.

Action is at the hub of every effective organisation, and the ability to know when to take action is another key characteristic of an effective leader. We all know someone who can 'talk the talk', i.e. they know all the right things to say and when to say them. But when it comes to converting their talk into action and start doing something, that's when their problems start. It is surprising the number of individuals, teams and organisations that set themselves up for failure by doing all the right things in terms of strategic and operational planning but then never actually take action. They plan to take account of every conceivable issue and look at all possibilities from all angles – they do every sense check, stress check and risk assessment they can think of – but ultimately they end up with paralysis by analysis. Consequently they plan themselves into oblivion and critically never take the first positive step to convert planning into action.

Action is about 'doing'. Some people prefer to be planners and some people prefer to be doers. Some people can be perceived as being impulsive, spontaneous, innovative and able to take the initiative. Others can be perceived as systematic, logical, persistent and even pedantic. There is a place for both because action without a framework of planning is dangerous, but planning with no subsequent action is a time-consuming and pointless exercise. If there is no apparent impact then what was the intended outcome of all the planning in the first place?

> *Effective leaders anticipate, plan and follow through with action.*

Leaders need to have a clear 'vision' and know the outcomes they want to achieve. Many will refer to 'goals' and implement action planning to illustrate how they intend to get there. However, goals are often too big to achieve in one step and therefore need to be broken down into a sequence of bite-size chunks, each with its own set of associated actions and measurable outcomes. Although this is obviously an effective strategy to map and manage the journey from start to finish, there is a danger that the individual stepping stones are implemented by different people in isolation meaning that the overall effect is fragmented and their contribution to the 'big picture' is lost. The most effective leaders will therefore realise that they often need to 'join the dots' to make sure that everyone involved appreciates the impact of their individual contribution on the final desired outcome.

If impact is a combination of planning and action then the secret is to get the balance right. Stephen Covey[4] highlighted this perfectly in his worldwide bestseller, *The Seven Habits of Highly Effective People*, by identifying the need for leaders to be proactive rather than reactive. In other words, effective leadership is about anticipating changing circumstances, recognising the potential threats and opportunities these can pose, then planning and acting accordingly. This again highlights the importance of anticipation linked to action as key behaviours in effective leadership.

---

4   Covey, Stephen, *The Seven Habits of Highly Effective People* (1989)

Attitude — Accept that it is your behaviour (and your response to others' behaviour) that is being perceived.

Anticipation — Learn from past mistakes and proactively use this knowledge to develop strategies, identify and recognise potential future scenarios.

Action — Plan carefully and know when to take action and convert planning into outcomes.

5

FIRMNESS – FAIRNESS
FLEXIBILITY

FIRMNESS

Keno was not happy! He obviously didn't understand what had happened to him or why he now had a plastic funnel on his head. The operation had been a success but he had a couple of wounds that needed time to heal. When the vet advised that I kept the cone on him twenty-four hours a day for ten days, I knew it was going to be difficult – it would take all my resolve to stand firm.

During the next ten days, Keno tried everything in his power to get me to take the cone off. He walked into walls and bashed it off doorways, which produced some incredibly sharp edges and turned it into a lethal weapon anytime he ran past someone's legs. He wedged it under the furniture and tried to pull it off, which left him with one ear bent at a strange angle for a couple of days. I'm sure he deliberately dribbled and dropped bits of food into it so that I spent most of my time cleaning it out for him. And when all this failed he simply sat and looked at me pathetically with his big brown eyes ...

I knew that my emotions were likely to drive my behaviour and therefore influence my actions. I also knew that, as a leader, I had to understand the reasons for my actions. This in turn would give me the reason to stand firm and would provide a framework in which I could control and manage my emotions. Consequently, despite the pleading eyes and regular Oscar-winning performances he put me through, I stood firm and Keno's cone stayed in place for ten days – a very long ten days.

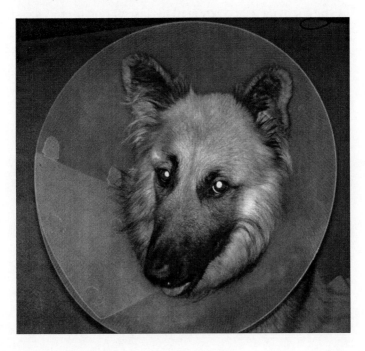

FAIRNESS

Dogs need consistency, especially in the early stages of their training. They need to know the rules and then learn that they will be applied in a fair and even-handed manner. Keno has always had a fascination (bordering on obsession) with socks – clean socks, dirty socks, ski socks, ankle socks – he doesn't care as long as it's a sock. As a puppy, I would find him snuffling around the washing basket or, worse still, standing with his head in Ken's work boots. Then he would dash out into the garden with his prized possession and by the time I recovered it, invariably the sock was full of holes. Ken has being going to work in odd socks for months but probably doesn't realise it!

As he got older, Keno retained his fascination for footwear but he now understands the rules and plays fairly. Most of the time he plays with typical 'dog' toys, all of which squeak of course. I then give him an odd sock as an occasional treat, which he carries around, sleeps with and basically attaches himself to for a period of twenty-four hours, and in return he refrains from helping himself if we leave any washing lying around. In the interim periods when a sock is not available, he has to make do with more typical toys.

FLEXIBILITY

By now I was confident that I was an effective leader and Keno was responding well. But, one of the biggest mistakes a leader can make is to assume that everybody around them thinks, processes and works in exactly the same way that they do. So, to explore this, I decided to carry out a simple experiment. My dog-walker went on holiday for a week and I volunteered to take over her dog-walking schedule. Apart from the obvious benefits of fresh air and exercise, this experience would bring me into contact with several different dogs, all of whom had their own personalities, quirks and characteristics that were distinctly different to Keno's. What I was trying to explore was whether the leadership approach that I used with Keno was transferable, or whether I needed to adapt and modify my skills to each individual dog.

I quickly identified that Becky (Springer Spaniel) was the energetic bundle of fun who lived life to the full but had the attention span of a doormat. Initially Becky got herself so excited at the thought of going for a walk that she would run around in circles and lose the plot completely! She had no concept of how to walk on a lead – she pulled permanently and did a passable impersonation of a Husky pulling a sledge.

With Becky, I had to constantly reinforce my position as 'pack leader'. Repetition and consistency of commands were essential here, and she responded very well. By the end of the week, I had established some clear rules and expectations and was confident enough to let her off the lead (in a secure enclosed space) knowing that she would return to me on command.

Simba (Rottweiler/Labrador cross) was the big, bulky Rambo-style dog that all passers-by gave a wide berth but he was really just a teddy bear with a mischievous sense of humour. He knew the effect he could have by curling his lip at people standing in the queue for the bus, which I'm sure he did deliberately!

Simba was very easy to walk and control. At first I thought this was because he was a similar size to Keno and I was simply used to a big dog. But gradually it became clear that Simba understood his role in our relationship and was perfectly comfortable with me exerting the power and taking the decisions.

Blue (Border Collie) was a classic follower – give him a stick and he would follow anyone to the end of the earth in the hope that one day they might actually throw it for him. I rarely had Blue on the lead because I knew he would never stray far from me and would come instantly the minute he was called. This trust was built on the fact that I simply had to pick up a stick and he would anticipate that I might play with him.

I have never had a female dog so was interested in how Millie (German Shepherd) would react and how similar she might be to Keno. Surprisingly, there were numerous occasions where her behaviour was so similar that I actually called her 'Keno' by mistake! She played in the same way that Keno did and always had to be the centre of attention. When Millie and Blue went out together, Millie always had to have the toy or stick – another trait shared with Keno – and she was always the first one back in the car to claim her space as soon as the door was opened.

So what did my dog walking experience teach me? I discovered that there were patterns and similarities in the way the different dogs responded. The skills I needed, however, remained the same and were transferable. I simply had to take time to calibrate each individual's behaviour and then be flexible in the way I approached working with them. Bringing together and leading a group of dogs was therefore no different to leading a group of people – by recognising the strengths and characteristics of each individual, and by consciously choosing to adapt my own behaviour and response, I became an effective leader and got the best out of each of them.

Leadership lessons

As a leader there are times when you will need to stand firm; to have the self-assurance, resolve and confidence to stand by your decisions and to draw the line across which people don't cross. Being firm is not about being a bully or about being overly aggressive. It is simply about standing your ground and making your position absolutely clear. Being firm isn't about getting your own way, digging your heels in and becoming obstinate in the face of disagreement with others. It is about clearly and rationally stating your position, explaining your underlying reasoning and then calmly and assertively stating what needs to be done as a result. Firmness is also not about power or domination. The 'do it because I told you to do it and I'm in charge' approach is not about being firm; this approach is more about using position and perceived authority rather than rational reason to influence and lead others.

The ability to stand firm comes from having the confidence and courage of your own convictions, and knowing that whatever decision you have made is well considered. It is therefore about having a belief in what you are asking of yourself and your colleagues, because without this belief you will unconsciously display physiological hints of hesitation and uncertainty. If you radiate anxiety and doubt when you are trying to stand firm, this will be perceived as weakness. If, however, you radiate calm assertive energy, this will be perceived as confidence and strength.

I am a great believer in 'mind over matter' when it comes to controlling the way you present yourself to others, and particularly when having to convey a message that might be unexpected or unpopular. Most leaders have informal 'Equity cards' and have learnt to create images of the traits they want to project, such as confidence, decisiveness and firmness. Think of the great leaders in the world of sport; they simply know the patterns of behaviour that they need to follow to be able to recreate the emotional responses they want to generate. This in turn leads to a physiological change that means their body language changes and they duly take on the characteristics that will help them succeed.

Beliefs and values are really powerful. If people don't believe in what they are doing, they simply won't do it effectively. Too often we make assumptions based on our own beliefs and values, and compound this with the incorrect assumption that everyone else is the same as us and therefore shares these.

> *Effective leaders understand the power of beliefs and values.*

This is why in any team it is critical to have a common understanding of the shared values and to be sure that these are congruent with the overall mission statement and vision of the organisation. This will then provide a framework within which the leadership will be perceived to be both firm and fair.

The most effective leaders are those who are seen as being fair, approachable and adaptable. Fairness is about treating others with honesty and respect, and considering their needs – treating others as you would wish to be treated yourself. However, being fair is more about being able to weigh up all the options and coming to reasoned decisions and arguments, rather than showing excessive empathy to the views and needs of others, which itself can cause further problems in the long run.

Consistency plays a big part in people's perceptions of fairness. Effective leaders are consistent in the way they behave and, as a result, people know what to expect and how to respond. This links back to everyone having a clear understanding of the various roles and responsibilities within their working group, and therefore knowing the rules, boundaries and limitations within which they are expected to perform.

Dogs regularly demonstrate flexibility in their behaviour. They guard and protect when they feel threatened, they play when they are happy and excited, and they withdraw when they are tired or unwell. These are common patterns of behaviour that are easily recognisable but then each animal has its own individual quirks and reactions that are unique. Generally speaking, a dog will approach each new person or situation as a blank canvas and will respond to the energy that it presents. This means that the behaviour the dog shows is typically a reflection of the energy that is being transmitted to it, rather than a habitual pattern that it runs. Humans, on the other hand, often repeat patterns of behaviour and approach situations in their preferred way rather than considering what would be the most appropriate behaviour and response to apply. As humans, we can learn a lot about flexibility and adaptability from our canine friends.

Flexibility is a fundamental skill for any leader. The ability to adapt to different circumstances and to be flexible in your own choice of behaviours will undoubtedly give you a winning edge. If you can develop the skill of being able to 'see' things from different perspectives you will give yourself a huge advantage, particularly in the areas of problem solving and decision making. I have worked with many leaders who have found that the simple technique of placing a hula hoop on the floor then stepping in and out of it (to view a problem from a different position) gives them a completely new perspective on an issue. This in turn changes the way they think about the problem and the strategies that they could use to tackle it.

> *Effective leaders have a broad repertoire of skills and behaviours and use them flexibly depending on the situation.*

Flexibility gives choice. This was recognised by Hersey and Blanchard in their classic Situational Leadership Model[5], where they basically stated that leadership is about having the repertoire of skills to adapt your styles and preferences to suit the situation, balancing the need to be supportive and/or directive. For instance, some situations may require a supportive coaching approach to help an individual achieve their objectives, while a different

---

5   Hersey, P., Blanchard, K., & Johnson, D. (2008). *Management of Organizational Behavior: Leading Human Resources* (9th ed.). Upper Saddle River, NJ: Pearson Education.

situation may need a more directive and tightly controlled approach.

Different situations will require different styles and approaches. This is basic common sense and most people do it naturally in their day-to-day lives, so why does it often appear to come as such a revelation to inexperienced leaders? To be an effective leader you need to have as broad a repertoire of skills and behaviours as possible, and have flexibility in the way you approach each situation.

The leader who has a high level of self-awareness and therefore knows his or her own strengths, limitations, preferences and habits, is the leader who will have the greatest potential to demonstrate flexibility in their choice and pattern of behaviour. Add in a good knowledge and understanding of the preferences and characteristics of the people they work with, and this leader has suddenly moved to a new level in being able to adapt and modify their leadership style to get the best from every situation. Unfortunately, too many leaders simply adopt their own preferred leadership style because it's the way they have always done it or they know no better.

Too few leaders really understand and exploit the power of profiling behaviour in the workplace, and therefore miss massive opportunities to develop and extend their flexibility and choice.

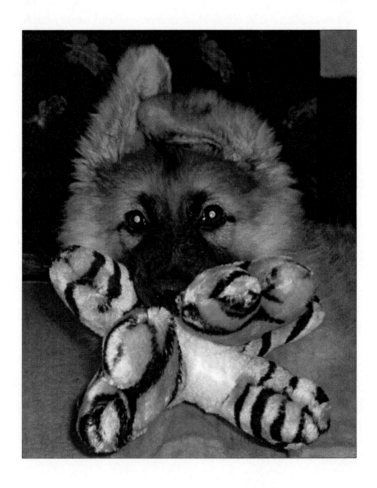

F irmness — Have the self-belief and resolve to stand your ground without resorting to aggressive behaviour.

F airness — Be consistent in your dealings with others – set clear boundaries and expectations.

F lexibility — Adapt and modify your own behaviour to suit the situation and get the best outcome for everyone concerned.

6

RECALL – REPETITION RESILIENCE

Recall

Because I am married to a police officer, I am regularly asked if Keno comes from police dog stock, which is highly amusing. Although he looks the part, Keno is so friendly and keen to please that he's more likely to lick a burglar to death than assist in an arrest! However, I had always known that he was a bright, intelligent dog and wondered just how he would react to the police's strict dog training regime. This is why one day I found myself standing on the edge of the training field watching Durham Constabulary's finest canine specimens being put through their paces on an agility obstacle course. Keno didn't seem particularly impressed and was apparently more interested in the rabbits that were foraging in the bushes than his supposed role models. But, as usual, I was wrong ...

About two weeks later I took Keno out for a late evening walk and decided to take a short cut home through the local children's park. The swings, roundabout and slide were empty and it was a lovely tranquil evening. Keno was off the lead and walking perfectly to heel until he suddenly took off like a bullet. What happened next was incredible. He ran up the metal steps of the slide and literally launched himself down the chute – precisely the way the police dogs had done during their training. Not only did he do it once but he made himself positively dizzy by repeating the manoeuvre several times and running back to me for praise at the end of each circuit.

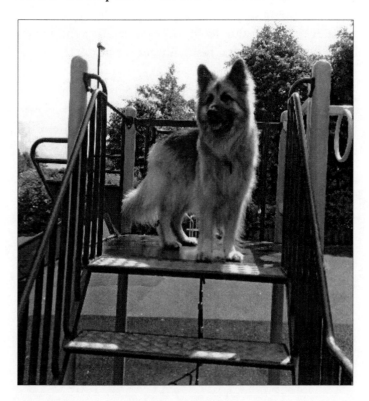

I had thought he wasn't paying any attention during our police visit but he had obviously remembered what to do and decided to wait and demonstrate his ability in his own time. He is now a regular in the park when there is no-one else around.

REPETITION

From day one, I have used single word commands with Keno. This way, he has learnt to respond to keywords and there can be no misinterpretation about what I expect him to do. For example, 'sit' produces an immediate reaction where he plonks his backside on the floor and poses proudly. 'Come' and 'fetch' were not so easy and took a little more practice but he finally got the gist of them.

Having witnessed too many examples of my Dad having to treat dogs who have been victims of road traffic accidents, I am very conscious about safety near roads and moving vehicles. I therefore taught Keno the 'road' and 'cross' commands while he was still a little puppy. Whenever we reached a kerb, 'road' was his signal to sit and remain in that position until told to 'cross'. I repeated these commands every day until I was confident he knew what to do and would respond to the command, regardless of who gave it to him. Now it was time to test my theory …

My repetition of keyword training and Keno's subsequent recall of the commands was perfect. The only problem was that Ken didn't quite use the commands in the same way I did. When he told Keno to 'sit' at the 'road', the dog did precisely that – he sat ('sit') and then refused to move ('road'). When Ken told him to 'come on' as he tried to drag him across the road, the dog remained impassive and firmly glued to the kerb. It took Ken over five minutes to coax him over to the other side, using treats and threats, by which time I was laughing helplessly at his efforts. I couldn't blame the dog – he had done exactly what he had been told to do and kept looking at me for encouragement. Maybe I need to think of a few choice keywords for Ken!

RESILIENCE

Keno loves water and indulges this passion at every possible opportunity. We live close to a river and several parks with lakes, which means he gets plenty of chances to get soggy. One of the parks is inhabited by several hundred ducks, various waterfowl and at least five breeding pairs of swans. It was only a matter of time before Keno fell foul of them, which he did spectacularly last summer.

It was a beautiful lazy Sunday morning and Keno was having a great game of 'chase' in the park with George (a one year old Boxer) when he ventured a little too close to the edge of the water and slipped unceremoniously into the lake. The resulting splash obviously frightened the birds – and the swans in particular – who took offence at their peace and quiet being shattered by thirty-eight kilos of damp dog. Things quickly went downhill from there as the swans positioned themselves between Keno and dry land. The ensuing battle of wills was quite remarkable; every time he tried to reach the water's edge, the swans blocked his path, so Keno simply kept trying to go round them until it became obvious they were not going to give way.

My resilient dog then decided to take the path of least resistance, swam the full length of the lake, and pranced back on dry land, stopping to bark victoriously at the swans as he passed.

LEADERSHIP LESSONS

Dogs are taught to 'recall' from an early age, i.e. they are taught to return to their owner on command. As any dog owner knows, this is not only an essential requirement but is one of the hardest things to achieve, especially when there are other distractions around that are infinitely more interesting than coming back to you!

Recall is the ability to recall knowledge, skills and understanding from previous experiences, and to apply them to the current situation. This in turn leads to the ability to learn from your mistakes and past experiences.

How do people learn to be leaders? Well, one of the most effective ways to establish positive skills and habits is to 'model' someone who already exhibits them. Simply identify their specific behaviours and characteristics, and subsequently the strategies that they use, then mimic and copy them. After all, this is how we learnt to walk and talk as children – we simply copied the other people around us and practised until we got it right. It may sound simplistic and too easy but genuine modelling takes time and practice. All the people

> *Effective leaders systematically model the behaviours of others and learn from them.*

who excel at sport know the benefits of effective modelling coupled with disciplined practice – just think of the term 'role model'.

Applying the same techniques to leadership will give you a really good starting point to apply and integrate a set of skills into your own repertoire once you know how someone else achieves the outcomes you want. So, if recall is about identifying where you have seen a skill, behaviour or characteristic being effective, and modelling is about eliciting the behaviours and strategies that the individual uses, who do you need to model, and why?

Repetition is simply practice, practice, practice. There is a constant argument about whether people are born natural leaders or whether leadership is something that can be learnt. Either way, it requires practice before the necessary skills and competences are embedded and become an instinctive and habitual part of your repertoire of behaviours.

Think about a time when you tried a new activity for the first time. Before you tried it, you probably had very little idea about how much you didn't know about the subject or topic. In other words, you were basically 'unconsciously incompetent'. As you started to gain a little knowledge and understanding, you probably became acutely aware of just how much you really didn't know. At this stage you became 'consciously incompetent' and were most likely to feel uncomfortable and possibly a little anxious or nervous about what you were doing and whether you were likely to succeed. This is the point in many situations where people typically give up and fail to complete their intended outcome. Sadly, this is often because they simply don't understand that it is an inevitable part of the learning curve and that further practice will lead to the development and improvement of skills.

Further practice and repetition would lead you to the 'consciously competent' stage where you knew what to do, but had to consciously think about what you were doing at the time. A classic example of this stage is the learner driver who has just passed their driving test. Once the euphoria dies down, they realise just how hard they still need to concentrate and focus when driving on the roads, especially now that other drivers are unlikely to show them the same tolerance!

Once behaviours have become an instinctive part of our everyday activities and routines, we have reached the final stage of 'unconsciously competent'. This is the stage where we not only know precisely what we have to do, and how to do it, but it almost becomes second nature and there is very little conscious energy or effort needed to complete the activity. Although this brings great benefits, it also brings the danger of habitual patterns forming. For example, a dog that was taught to chase sticks when it was puppy will still pick up sticks and encourage you to throw them as an adult dog – not because it doesn't know any better but because it simply runs the same pattern of behaviour every time it sees a stick. Now

> *Effective leaders are aware of their own habits and recognise the impact of their behaviours and actions.*

ask yourself what behavioural patterns do you run habitually and how well do they serve you as a leader?

Effective leaders have a capacity to absorb energy (both positive and negative) and to use this creatively to avoid issues, problems and detrimental impacts. This resilience is a fundamental part of any leader's make-up if they are going to be able to handle and manage personal and professional stress. That is not to say that leaders don't get stressed, but it is the way they respond to stressors and manage their own internal emotional states that sets the best leaders apart. Understanding your own emotional intelligence, and the way you will respond in different situations, is one of the most important skills you will ever learn.

Many of today's most inspirational business leaders and entrepreneurs have failed at something at some stage previously in their lives. Their resilience and ability to 'bounce back' is often the distinguishing feature between them and others, coupled with their ability to recall and subsequently anticipate future situations. You can guarantee they won't make the same mistake twice!

Recall — Apply your previous knowledge, skills and understanding to current situations.

Repetition — Practise until the skills and competences you require are instinctive and habitual.

Resilience — Manage your own emotional state and learn to bounce back from disappointment.

7

Conflict – Compromise Collaboration

Conflict

Toby is a Golden Labrador cross – he is also Keno's arch enemy. This wouldn't be too bad if it wasn't for the fact that Toby lives close by and walks past our house several times a day, which is the catalyst for World War III to break out at our living room window. Toby attacked Keno when he was a puppy – he actually missed the dog and bit me causing a wound that needed medical attention – so I can fully understand why there is an ongoing conflict, particular as Keno has grown up and assumed his role as protector and guard dog.

Unfortunately, for a period of time, Keno seemed unable (or unwilling) to distinguish between Toby and any other Golden Retriever, which became particularly embarrassing as he would literally launch himself at every one he met. The interesting thing was that he only did this with me; he obviously assumed that Ken could look after himself.

There are bound to be certain dogs that Keno simply doesn't like or want to socialise with, but this ongoing conflict was creating a situation that could potentially escalate further – I had to do something about it. My answer was to enlist the help of a friend and her docile Golden Retriever, Andrex. Having discussed the situation, we decided to tackle the issue head-on. We simply took the dogs to the beach (in separate cars) and waited until there was no-one else around then let them both off their leads. After an initial brief tussle, which sounded much worse than it looked, Andrex and Keno lost interest in each other and became more excited about chasing seagulls and playing in the waves. In this instant, I realised that I had relaxed my shoulders and was much calmer in myself and that Keno had responded positively to the change in my demeanour and was now playing happily with his new friend. Thinking back to all the times we had encountered Toby, I realised that I had always tensed and radiated anxiety, so was it any wonder that Keno reacted the way he did? Since this day, I make a conscious effort to remain calm whenever Toby is around. Keno's behaviour has improved dramatically although he still growls and spits at him occasionally just to keep up appearances!

Compromise

Keno is not allowed upstairs. Right from the start, I had been adamant that he did not come into the bedrooms and most certainly did not sleep on the beds. When he was little he couldn't climb the stairs anyway, so the issue only raised its head when it got to the point where he was big enough to climb and started to explore. We seem to have reached a reasonable compromise. He will come half-way up and balance precariously on the sixth step – something he managed easily when he was a puppy but has become increasingly difficult as he has grown.

Following our power struggle over access to our leather sofas, imagine my surprise when I walked in to my mum's house one day to find Keno blatantly lounging on her furniture! My first reaction was to throw him off and reprimand him until I realised that my Mum was sitting chatting away to him; he had clearly been given permission and had no intention of moving for me. Again, common sense prevailed and I accepted that I had to compromise. We now both know that there are different rules in the different houses, which we respect and abide by.

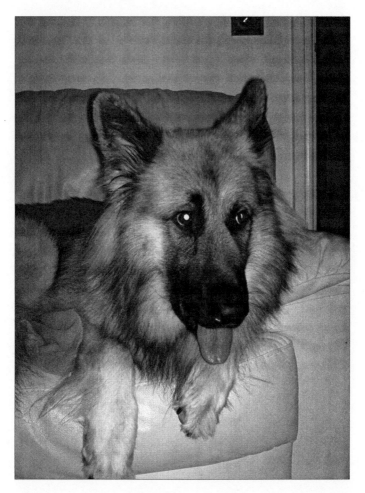

COLLABORATION

Before I finally got it under control, Keno's aggression towards Toby (and any Toby lookalikes) was beginning to worry me so I decided to take him to training classes to give him the chance to mix and socialise with other dogs. Typically, he was the star of the show! If I gave him a command, he did it immediately then looked around for approval. If I left him in a sitting or lying position, he remained like a perfect statue until I returned. I even taught him to 'dance' and he performed like one of the cast of *Fame*! Obviously our partnership was working well and our collaboration was meeting both our needs. I was demonstrating that I could control a dog and he was illustrating that he was perfectly capable of following my lead, albeit only when it suited him.

So, since I often walk Keno in a dark unlit area at night, I decided to practise a new command – 'guard' – expecting him to protect me. As you can see, he obviously hasn't quite got the hang of this one yet!

LEADERSHIP LESSONS

Dogs rarely go out looking for a fight. What we perceive as aggressive behaviour is often a dog's way of claiming and controlling its space or territory. Dogs do this by projecting energy that psychologically lets others around know their intention. This is typically accompanied by body language clues and eye contact that reinforce the message. Humans work in exactly the same way but are sometimes not so subtle!

The word 'conflict' often evokes images of people in direct aggression with each other. This needn't be the case and in all organisations a degree of conflict is not only necessary but likely to do some good. For instance, does having conflicting views mean that you cannot work with another person? Does having different, conflicting ideas and opinions automatically mean that one of you is right and the other therefore has to be wrong? Conflict simply means that there is a difference or variance between two things – it needn't become a contradiction, argument or dispute if handled appropriately.

There is no need for conflict to become unpleasant or unhelpful although it will undoubtedly at times be uncomfortable. So the message for an effective leader is to anticipate when, and why, conflict could occur and to have appropriate strategies in place to handle it and to manage the situation to ensure that everybody has the opportunity to air their differing views, opinions and ideas without any aggression coming to the fore.

> *Effective leaders anticipate where conflict could occur and harness this to support constructive problem solving and decision making.*

A certain degree of conflict is healthy. After all, if we all held similar views, opinions and ideas then it wouldn't exactly stimulate interesting or creative discussions in the workplace, would it? Imagine a world where everyone agreed with you all the time. Healthy conflict is also essential for decision making and problem solving. An effective leader will use a situation where conflict could occur to create a framework in which people can bounce their own ideas off each other in a non-threatening, constructive and supportive way. They will create the environment for this to happen and will also anticipate the potential outcomes (and potential objections) from the individuals concerned. The most effective leaders will have appropriate responses already prepared to tackle and diffuse any issues that could escalate into unhealthy and harmful conflict. This again reinforces the key requirement for a leader to be able to 'anticipate' before they can lead or manage other people.

Damaging and detrimental conflict happens when a leader simply doesn't create the correct environment and therefore allows individuals to take control of the situation, often leading to disagreement. This is where personal views, feelings and potential prejudices can escalate into what is perceived as an aggressive and detrimental situation. This inevitably leads to the 'I win – you lose' situation where aggressive and competitive behaviour comes to the fore.

When human beings are brought together for extended periods of time (e.g. in the typical workplace) there is an inevitability that a certain degree of conflict will occur. Conflict is often the end result of clashes in personality or 'attitude' or style or approach, all of which can very easily be explained in one simple word – behaviour. So, the more a leader understands the behavioural characteristics, preferences and styles, not only of themselves but of the individuals for whom they are responsible and work with on a regular basis, the more effective that leader will be in being able to adapt, modify and change their behaviour to create the most conducive environment for productive working and to anticipate and minimise the impact of conflict.

The ability to compromise is a key strength in any individual, and particularly a leader, although some people still perceive any situation where they do not exert their authority to 'get their own way' as a potential weakness. This is a common mistake that inexperienced leaders often make; trying to use their position and perceived status to drive decisions and actions rather than their skills and behaviours to work with, and through, their people.

It would be unhealthy if we each got our own way all the time. Again, imagine a world where you never disagreed with someone else, didn't have to justify or rationalise your arguments, and all your ideas and suggestions were accepted on face value. Where is the fun and challenge in that? Clearly, there is a need for compromise in any situation or organisation where there is more than one person involved. Compromise is about finding a 'win-win' situation, particularly when speed is concerned or the issue itself is of low risk or value to you and others involved.

> *Effective leaders recognise and understand the influence of the behavioural characteristics, preferences and styles of themselves and others they work with.*

Compromise is about finding the middle ground. Therefore, a leader who can create opportunities for win-win situations without conceding their own position will be skilled in the art of influence and persuasion. They may well be perceived as being accommodating and lenient, which in itself brings potential strengths or perceived liabilities. However, the art of compromise is a fundamental skill for any leader to get the best from their people.

One of the biggest mistakes a leader can make is to assume that everybody around them thinks, processes and works in exactly the same way that they do. The most effective leaders appreciate the significant differences among their people and capitalise on these to get the best out of each individual. This can often mean adapting their own views or approach to meet the needs of others, i.e. to give and take (compromise).

In the 1970's, Kenneth Thomas and Ralph Kilman identified five basic ways of addressing conflict and subsequently developed their TKI Conflict Mode Instrument[6], which is widely used to assess an individual's behaviour in conflict situations. Their work centred around the concept that a person's behaviour will be governed by two basic factors: 'assertiveness' and 'cooperativeness'. Depending on the balance of these two dimensions, Thomas and Kilman characterised five conflict handling modes, each of which has its uses. For a leader, the important message is that we are capable of using all

---

6   Thomas-Kilman Conflict Mode Instrument, 1974, Xicom Incorporated, CPP Inc.

five modes but are likely to have natural preferences; consequently we will tend to rely more heavily on some behaviours than others when facing a conflict situation. The effective leader will recognise the situation and adapt their mode of behaviour accordingly to achieve the correct outcome.

Collaboration is the ultimate situation where people work together to find a solution that satisfies all their needs. Genuine collaboration can reap massive benefits for an organisation but is hard to achieve. People will not work together effectively if they do not have a shared understanding of the common goals they are trying to achieve and if their individual needs outweigh the group outcome. Crucially, true collaboration will only be effective when the individuals concerned have 'shared' values.

The whole area of values is one that a leader needs to consider very carefully. Put simply, values are the things that drive each individual and make them take the decisions and actions they do. If something goes against your values, it will feel wrong and you will be uncomfortable. When people have shared values, there will be a degree of congruence and compatibility. They probably can't define it and don't know why – that is the power of your values.

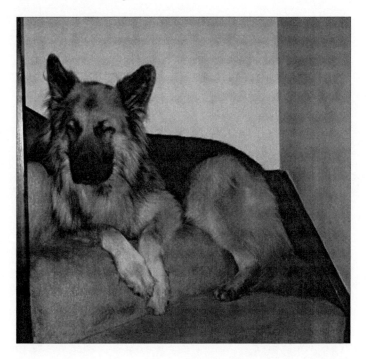

C onflict   Anticipate and have strategies in place to make conflict healthy and beneficial.

C ompromise   Accept other's similarities and differences and adapt your behaviour to get the best win-win solutions.

C ollaboration   Make sure there are shared values and understanding so that everyone can contribute in their own way.

8

Intuition – Influence Intention

Intuition

The first time Keno met Ken's mum was wonderful to watch. She is quite elderly and a long-term disability has left her very unsteady on her feet. He showed his usual puppy exuberance as he bounded towards her standing in the doorway. At that precise moment, an image of ten-pin bowling flashed through my mind as I imagined my mother-in-law lying prone on the hall floor with a bouncing puppy sitting astride her.

To my amazement, Keno's 100 metre dash rapidly slowed as he applied the brakes and came to a skidding halt at Marjorie's feet. He sat perfectly, looked up at her adoringly and gently rested his head against her walking stick.

What had made him do this? How did he know that she was so frail and likely to fall? I have to believe that some form of intuition kicked in and that the dog sensed Marjorie's vulnerability. This clearly affected his actions and he responded to her in the most appropriate way.

Since that first meeting, they have had a bond that is clear for everyone to see. He slows down around her, is gentle in the way he moves past her and regularly lies at her feet as if protecting her.

Influence

Keno's behaviour around other dogs has improved significantly to the point that I am now perfectly comfortable letting him run around off the lead and play with other dogs. I have overcome my concern about his unpredictability and he is a much happier and more sociable dog as a result. So what brought about this change of behaviour? Basically, I realised that I was actually the biggest part of the problem! I had got into the habit of anticipating trouble and therefore I was becoming tense and anxious whenever other dogs were around. Keno was picking this up and mirroring my emotional state, which meant that he was feeling uncomfortable and potentially vulnerable. He then simply reacted in the only way he knew how, which was to become aggressive and confrontational with the other dogs. The minute I relaxed and took on a more positive and calm approach, he did the same.

I am amazed at my ability to influence Keno's manner and behaviour, simply by changing my own state. For instance, he is now quite happy to sit and watch other dogs running and playing until I give him permission to join in. He will share his toys with other dogs (whereas he would previously have been overprotective of his tennis ball) and he happily chases sticks and trots back without it when someone else gets there first. Yet he knows when I feel threatened or uncomfortable and still reacts accordingly. For example, we recently came face to face with a huge and rather ugly looking Husky that was clearly having a bad day! The Husky took one look at me and growled menacingly, which Keno took as his cue. He positioned himself firmly between me and the other dog, stood stock still, arched his back and snarled menacingly. I knew instantly that one possible outcome was a nasty fight that I didn't want to be in the middle of, so the impact of my ability to influence Keno was going to be crucial in getting the right result. I was impressed by his protectiveness (and rather sinister snarl) but was even more impressed by his immediate response when I calmly stepped aside and told him to 'lie down' and 'stay'. He hit the ground immediately and lay patiently while the other owner put her dog on the lead, apologised for his aggression and literally dragged him off in the opposite direction.

I had to laugh as I heard her admonishing her dog and saying, "Why can't you be as well behaved as that lovely dog?" If only she knew!

Intention

It was a beautiful sunny afternoon and Keno was lying happily sunbathing in Marjorie's back garden when my nephew arrived, complete with his new acquisition – Swingball. For the first few minutes Keno continued to lie quietly as if he didn't have a care in the world, but I knew from his subtle movements and the glint in his eyes that he was gearing himself up for action. I watched entranced as his body language changed ever so slowly from a relaxed, prone, lounging position to one where he had all the coiled anticipation of a predator stalking its unsuspecting prey (in this case the innocent tennis ball on the end of the rope).

His intention was becoming abundantly clear – there was no doubt. He was going to have that tennis ball!

Since this experience, I have seen the same pattern of behaviour in Keno in a number of different situations where he has geared himself up for action. The signs had been there all the time in his body language and eye movements, but I hadn't noticed them. All I have to do now is recognise some of the subtle changes in his behaviour and movements to know his intention.

LEADERSHIP LESSONS

The higher you get up the leadership ladder, the worse the vulnerability gets. I have lost count of the number of times some of my clients in senior leadership positions have expressed their fears and concerns, such as, "I'm just waiting for the day when I get found out. You know, the

measured against the impact it is likely to have so that everyone is clear about the outcomes that can be expected and why this would be of benefit.

The easiest way to assess impact is by asking a simple question: "So what? If I take this course of action, then so what?". If the answer is unclear or cannot easily be expressed then there is more thought needed before moving on. Effective leadership is about not only assessing risk prior to taking decisions and actions but is also about having sufficient mechanisms, controls, checks and balances in place to be able to measure the impact of those decisions and actions. Crucially, by mapping out (and articulating) the expectations in advance, leaders will be better placed to recognise when things are not progressing as planned and therefore be able to intervene and change direction more effectively. Unfortunately, too often leaders embark on courses of action because "that's the way it's always been done around here" and then miraculously express surprise that they get a similar result or outcome to the last time!

> *Effective leaders understand the power of questions and active listening.*

If influence is about being able to sell your ideas, views and concepts to others, and being in a position to anticipate and articulate the outcomes that can be expected, it is therefore about listening to, and soliciting others' ideas and opinions, while putting forward a convincing argument. The ability to influence requires the key skill of being able to listen – not just being able to hear, but to listen actively at a range of levels.

Leaders need to listen to the words, to the meaning, to the feeling, and to the intent. Only when you understand the emotion sitting behind somebody's behaviour and words will you fully understand what it is that is motivating them. The most effective leaders then exert influence by hitting the correct motivational 'hot spots', balanced with the integrity to avoid each individual's inherent fears.

The human brain processes information faster than our mouths work, which means that we can think much faster than we can speak. Although this is a useful trait, it typically means that we are busy thinking about what the other person has said and are likely to be formulating what we are going to say next, while they are still speaking. The danger here is that we then don't listen carefully enough and only pick up part of their message. Active listening involves slowing down the process where our personal filters, assumptions, judgements, and beliefs can distort what we hear. The simplest way to do this is to ask questions, which requires a conscious effort to reflect on what has been said and to check for understanding.

Having the ability to understand the intention behind someone else's words or actions is a critical skill for a leader to develop. The good news is that people are signposting their intentions all the time, through the language they choose to use and the way they express their emotions through their behaviour. Like modelling, learning to 'read' and interpret the cues in someone's speech patterns, facial expressions and body movements are skills that can be learnt and developed over time.

I ntuition   Learn to trust your gut instinct – if it feels right there is a good reason why.

I nfluence   Understand the impact of your actions and adapt your behaviours accordingly.

I ntention   Listen for the intention and motivation rather than what you want to hear.

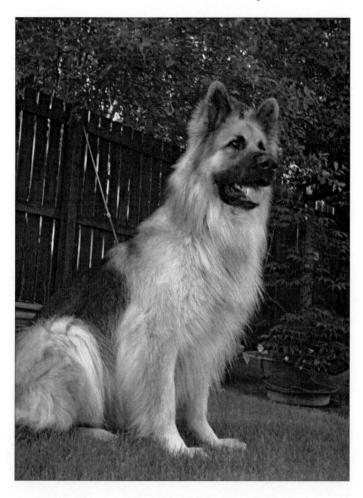

9

A BLUEPRINT FOR LEARNING TO LEAD

Position	Power	Persuasion
Always be the 'pack leader'	Know what you are trying to achieve and believe in it and yourself	Be flexible and adaptable in your own behaviour
Roles	Responsibilities	Relationships
Be clear about each individual's purpose, function and contribution to the team	Communicate responsibilities (and boundaries) clearly to everyone in the team	Anticipate factors that could affect relationships and clarify your expectations

Attitude	Anticipation	Action
Accept that it is your behaviour (and your response to others' behaviour) that is being perceived	Learn from past mistakes and proactively use this knowledge to develop strategies, identify and recognise potential future scenarios	Plan carefully and know when to take action and convert planning into outcome
Firmness	**Fairness**	**Flexibility**
Have the self-belief and resolve to stand your ground without resorting to aggressive behaviour	Be consistent in your dealings with others – set clear boundaries and expectations	Adapt and modify your own behaviour to suit the situation and get the best outcome for everyone concerned
Recall	**Repetition**	**Resilience**
Apply your previous knowledge, skills and understanding to current situations	Practise until the skills and competences you require are instinctive and habitual	Manage your own emotional state and learn to bounce back from disappointment

Conflict	Compromise	Collaboration
Anticipate and have strategies in place to make conflict healthy and beneficial	Accept others' similarities and differences and adapt your behaviour to get the best win-win solutions	Make sure there are shared values and understanding so that everyone can contribute in their own way
Intuition	Influence	Intention
Learn to trust your gut instinct – if it feels right there is a good reason why	Understand the impact of your actions and adapt your behaviours accordingly	Listen for the intention and motivation rather than what you want to hear

10

LEADERSHIP LESSONS

Dogs need strong leadership – they need rules and boundaries to be set so that they know precisely how they are expected to respond and behave – people are no different.

In fact, the parallels between canine and human needs are remarkable and if you look around you will see that people also behave in a similar way to dogs. Give them too much latitude and leeway and they will take advantage of it; control them too tightly and they will rebel and fight against the oppression they perceive. We can learn a lot about effective leadership from our canine companions ...

So what are the key lessons that I have learned from my experiences with Keno?

- 🐾 Trying to 'manage' won't work. Leadership and management are different and, to be a leader, I need a completely different set of skills.

- 🐾 My expectations must be clear at all times.

- 🐾 Anticipation is the key factor in effective leadership. The ability to anticipate gives me an edge and allows me to plan and prepare accordingly.

- 🐾 My emotional state has a huge influence on my behaviour and response to situations, which affects how others respond to me (even if they don't realise it at the time).

- 🐾 All the information I need is there in body language, habits and patterns of behaviour. I just have to recognise and interpret it to make it work for me.

- 🐾 Consciously making small and subtle changes in my behaviour can have dramatic effects.

- 🐾 There is no such thing as 'attitude' – only behaviour that I either like or don't like.

- 🐾 Modelling is marvellous! After all, why reinvent the wheel? If someone else is effective at something then I can learn from them.

It's not as hard as it looks! By cutting through all the theory and putting simple steps into practice, I am improving my leadership skills every day.

But the more important question should really be ... *what has Keno taught you?*

🐾 ....

🐾 ....

🐾 ....

🐾 ....

🐾 ....

🐾 ....

🐾 ....

🐾 ....

🐾 ....

🐾 ....

🐾 ....

Who Put You in Charge?

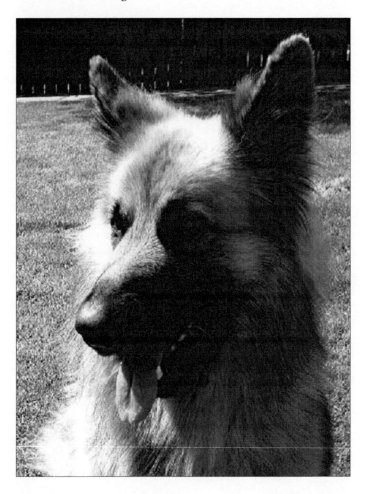

References

Full details of the models and techniques mentioned in this book can be found in the footnote references stated. Here is a simplified overview of each intended purely for quick reference.

Tuckman's Team Development Model (page 22)

Tuckman identified four stages in team development: forming – storming – norming – performing. Each stage is characterised by a set of behaviours within the team and therefore needs a different style and approach to leadership to maintain and promote development.

Forming:
This is the first stage of team building where the individual members meet and learn about the opportunity and challenges facing them. They will agree on goals for the

team and begin to tackle the tasks but, although they are likely to be motivated to work together, the team members will invariably behave independently. People will be on their best behaviour but will focus on themselves rather than the team. In the forming stage, a leader must set a clear direction for the team. Anticipation comes in here too – an effective leader will know that the team will inevitably enter the next (storming) stage as it develops and will therefore be prepared for it.

Storming:
This is the stage where team members begin to challenge and question, hence 'storming' which is often the result. Confrontation and conflict often happen as individuals vie for position and cliques and alliances typically form where people align themselves with like-minded individuals. Some teams come through this stage quickly but others can get stuck here and remain storming, which is clearly destructive in the long run. In the storming stage, a leader must reinforce the team's objectives and define clear expectations for behaviour. The ability to understand different perspectives, appreciate different views, and recognise that team members may be trying to establish their roles, responsibilities and 'identity' is crucial to the effective leadership of a team at this stage.

Norming:
When a team enters the norming stage they have established rules, boundaries and expectations, and will start to behave accordingly. Although trust and motivation often increase, there is a danger that habits form and 'group think' starts to take over from individual creativity within the team. In the

norming stage, a leader should shift focus to the decision making and problem solving strategies used by the team and will start delegating more responsibility. Anticipation comes in again as a key aspect because an effective leader will always be watching for any factors that could flip the team back into the storming phase. Examples are typically a change in personnel, either someone leaving or joining the team, or external threats and influences. The effective leader will anticipate and plan for any such circumstances with the aim of preventing, or at least minimising, the impact of reverting to storming.

Performing:
Some teams will reach the performing stage where they function smoothly and effectively as a unit. At this stage, team members have become inter-dependent and the identity of the team is recognised. In the performing stage, a leader will participate in the work of the team and will contribute to the decision making process. Effective leadership becomes a challenge to anticipate and proactively seize opportunities and plan for change.

Blake Mouton Grid Model (page 25)

This model represents two factors on a grid and attributes different leadership styles to different positions on the grid. The X-axis represents 'concern for production' (i.e. the outcomes) and the Y-axis represents 'concern for people'.

People

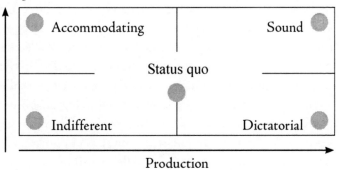

Production

The indifferent (impoverished) style is where there is an equally low concern for both people and production. In this situation, the main concern is often job security and not being held accountable for mistakes. This is not an effective approach to leadership and would lead to stagnation and lack of innovation.

The accommodating (country club) style typically creates a friendly and comfortable working environment with strong relationships. However, there is low concern for production and the outcomes typically suffer. This style of leadership does not consistently promote or challenge performance.

The dictatorial (produce or perish) style is characterised by control and domination. The achievement of goals and targets is paramount and this leadership style is typically evident in crisis management situations.

The status quo (middle of the road) style achieves a balance between workers' needs and company goals. However, the result of compromising for both people and production is often mediocre performance, which can become accepted as the norm. The danger of this approach is that complacency can set in and leadership does not anticipate and respond quickly enough to change.

The sound (team) style encourages team work and commitment. By adopting this approach, the leadership is effective; it recognises and satisfies the needs of the workers while striving for high output. The leader will not be frightened to challenge under-performance and will have all the necessary skills to motivate, influence, anticipate change and sustain production.

Johari Window (page 35)

The Johari Window was devised as a cognitive psychological tool to be used in an exercise to help people understand their interpersonal relationships and communications. Used in this context, an individual and their peers would place fifty-six specified adjectives in different positions on a grid to represent the individual's behaviour and motives. One key outcome is to identify the 'blind spots' where the individual is unaware of their traits and characteristics, and to then plan for future development.

I prefer to think of Johari's Window as a window with four panes of glass. Each pane represents the behaviours that are known to either yourself and/or others. The panes will therefore differ in size depending on who you are interacting with at any given time and how well they know you.

Open window	Blind window
This represents what you know about yourself and have shared with the other person, so they know about you.	This represents what the other person knows about you but you don't know i.e. their perceptions of you, judgements, etc
Closed window	Hidden window
This represents what you know about yourself but have not shared with the other person.	This represents what you don't even know about yourself yet.

The key to understanding Johari's Window is that information can be moved from one pane to another. This happens either when someone volunteers information i.e. they 'tell' or 'feedback' to someone, or when someone elicits information by 'asking'. For example, if I chose to tell you something about me that you didn't already know, then this would move from my hidden window to my open window. Alternatively the same result could be achieved by you asking me a question and me giving you an answer.

In a work situation, the most important window for a leader to be aware of is the 'blind' window. This is where people store their perceptions and judgements about other people. It is also where an individual may be 'blind' to their behaviours and their impact. An effective leader will recognise and appreciate this and ensure that appropriate mechanisms are in place to provide feedback to the individual concerned.

The Seven Habits of Highly Effective People (page 38)

Stephen Covey's renowned publication is based on the premise that values govern people's behaviour, but principles ultimately determine the consequences. By identifying a series of seven 'habits' and linking them to effectiveness, Covey provided a basic framework for leaders to model.

Habit 1: Be proactive
This habit explores personal choice, accepting that you are in charge and expanding your circle of influence to recognise and capitalise on opportunities.

Habit 2: Begin with the end in mind
This habit explores the need to understand your core values and have a clear outcome to aim for (personal vision) in order to set a direction for action.

Habit 3: Put first things first
This habit explores self-disciple and management in order to organise, delegate and exert independent will.

Habit 4:Think Win/Win
This habit explores the focus on people and problems, and advocates adopting a win/win frame of mind at all times.

Habit 5: Seek first to understand, then to be understood
This habit explores the essence of rapport and the need to develop empathetic listening skills.

Habit 6: Synergize
This habit explores the principles of creative co-operation and mutual gain.

Habit 7: Sharpen the saw
This habit explores the need to take time out of activities for personal well-being.

<u>Situational Leadership</u> (page 50)

Hersey and Blanchard identified four behavioural leadership styles in terms of the amount of direction and support that the leader provides to their followers. They named them S1 to S4.

S1: Directing/Telling
Using this style, a leader will define the roles and tasks, make the decisions and communicate to others by 'directing' or 'telling' them what to do. There will be little consultation and tight control of processes and procedures.

S2: Coaching/Selling
Using this style, a leader will still define the roles and tasks and make the decisions. However, they will seek ideas and suggestions, and communication is more of a two-way process.

S3: Supporting/Participating
Using this style, a leader will take part in decisions but more in the role of a facilitator. The allocation of tasks, management of processes and control is usually passed to others.

S4: Delegating

Using this style, a leader will still be involved in critical processes, such as problem solving, but others will decide when and how the leader needs to be involved in day-to-day activities.

Everyone will have their own natural style and preference. However, effective leaders need to be flexible and have the ability to adapt themselves according to the needs of the situation.

Thomas-Kilman Conflict Mode Instrument (page 72)

The Thomas-Kilman Conflict Mode Instrument (TKI) assesses an individual's behaviour in conflict situations. It considers the extent to which an individual attempts to satisfy his or her own concerns (assertiveness) balanced against the extent to which they attempt to satisfy the other person's concerns (cooperativeness).

From answering thirty questions, the result is a graph indicating the repertoire of conflict handling modes typically used by that individual. This illustrates their preferred choice and dominant behaviours in conflict situations.

Competing:	Assertive and uncooperative
Collaborating:	Assertive and cooperative
Compromising:	Intermediate in assertiveness and cooperativeness
Avoiding:	Unassertive and uncooperative
Accommodating:	Unassertive and cooperative

Each mode has its uses and an effective leader will anticipate and recognise conflict situations as they occur and have the adaptability to select the most appropriate conflict handling mode for the situation.

Neuro-linguistic programming (page 81)

Neuro-linguistic programming (NLP) is based on a theoretical connection between neurological processes (neuro), language patterns (linguistic) and behavioural patterns that have been learned through experience (programming).

The key principle is that once these patterns are isolated, and any relevant strategies associated with them are clearly defined, an individual can organise

The principle of modelling is a core element of NLP. By eliciting the strategies that a successful individual uses to carry out a task or activity, it is possible to identify specific factors that can be then be transferred and 'modelled' to create a similar experience in another person.

ABOUT THE AUTHOR

Lesley Hunter is a professional trainer with particular
expertise, and first-hand
experience, in developing
leadership skills. After
graduating as a microbiologist,
she qualified as a teacher
working in secondary
education then as a senior
lecturer in one of the largest
Colleges in the UK. Her
career further developed during her time at a County
Council in the North East of England, with a range of
responsibilities linked to teaching, learning and leadership
development.

Aged just 33, Lesley left behind the comfort and security
of full-time employment to set up her first business,
working predominantly with senior leaders in education
whilst fulfilling the demanding role of lead inspector of
schools. Expanding further with international clients,
Lesley's reputation for entrepreneurship and challenging
leadership thinking began to take shape. Since then, she
has been involved in the operational development of several
business ventures through which she has amassed a wide
range of leadership skills. Lesley has therefore learned the
practical aspects of business development and growth from
personal experience. This includes making some pretty
impressive mistakes along the way!

In 2005, Lesley decided there was more to life than being "the boss" and made a conscious decision to radically change her lifestyle. She walked away from all her business interests and immersed herself in a programme of personal development. She also bought a puppy!

Lesley now works exclusively for herself and specialises in helping people understand how behaviour lies at the heart of effective leadership, communication and performance. She is a regular public speaker and her seminars and workshops are renowned for challenging and motivating people from all walks of life.

Lesley has always had dogs in her life, from her early childhood experiences with the family's mischievous Cairn Terrier to her current companion, and the inspiration for this book, a high spirited, independent and stubborn German Shepherd called Keno.

Lightning Source UK Ltd.
Milton Keynes UK
16 May 2010

154237UK00001B/10/P